Good People

Michaela Whit —
With much
love & gratitude —
you are good
People!
Allison

Allison Zimmerman

Trilogy Christian Publishers A Wholly Owned Subsidary of Trinity Broadcasting Network 2442 Michelle Drive Tustin, CA 92780

First Trilogy Christian Publishing hardcover edition May 2018 Trilogy Christian Publishing/ TBN and colophon are trademarks of Trinity Broadcasting Network.

For information about special discounts for bulk purchases, please contact Trilogy Christian Publishing.

Manufactured in the United States of America

10 9 8 7 6 5 4 3 2 1

Library of Congress Cataloging-in-Publication Data is available.

ISBN 978-1-64088-091-7 (Paperback)
ISBN 978-1-64088-092-4 (ebook)

Dedicated to
Lynn, with gratitude

Look for the Posie-Angel, she is hiding on the pages.
How many Posie-Angels can you find?

Respectful people are
good people.
Good people
are people
you can respect.

2

Good people listen.
Good people care.
Good people believe children.

Good people play games
and have fun.

5

Good people respect each other.
Good people <u>respect</u>
each other's <u>bodies.</u>
What's yours is <u>yours.</u>
What's mine is <u>mine.</u>

Good people don't make you keep secrets.

Good people don't take you
away from the group to
touch you.

Good people don't touch what is yours.
Or make
you touch
what is theirs.

13

Good people
don't make you
do scary things.

Good people
don't tell you
not to tell
or
to "keep it a secret."

Good people trust each other.
Good people believe
each other.

Good people care for each other.
Good people will never touch you in a way that makes you feel bad
-that is not good.

You are a
good person.
You are kind,
you are brave,
you tell the truth.
I believe you!

21

You are allowed to say "No."

Good people will listen.
Your voice is good.
It is a gift from God.

About the Author

Allison, mother of 5, grandmother of 6, along with her husband Rob, has spent her life story in the Pacific Islands. In 2015 she was called away from the lands she loved to care for her son who was crushed and left for dead in a hit and run. Her son continues to make a miraculous recovery. Allison's journey is one that has seen the power of God to heal from the inside out. It is from this wealth that she writes.

9 781640 880917